AF269855

BOB DYLAN

BOB DYLAN

Celebrated Singer-Songwriter

Matt Doeden

LERNER PUBLICATIONS ◆ MINNEAPOLIS

Lerner Publications Company
An imprint of Lerner Publishing Group, Inc.
241 First Avenue North
Minneapolis, MN 55401 USA

For reading levels and more information, look up this title at www.lernerbooks.com.

Main body text set in Rotis Serif Std.
Typeface provided by Adobe Systems.

Editor: Ashley Kuehl **Designer:** Lauren Cooper **Photo Editor:** Lucien Brinkley

Library of Congress Cataloging-in-Publication Data

Names: Doeden, Matt, author.
Title: Bob Dylan : celebrated singer-songwriter / Matt Doeden.
Description: Minneapolis : Lerner Publications, 2025. | Series: Gateway biographies | Includes
   bibliographical references and index. | Audience: Ages 9–14 | Audience: Grades 4–6 |
   Summary: "Bob Dylan is known as the voice of his generation. Readers uncover Dylan's
   fascinating life story as well as the incredible songs and revolutionary lyrics that have helped
   shape American musical history"– Provided by publisher.
Identifiers: LCCN 2024055927 (print) | LCCN 2024055928 (ebook) | ISBN 9798765669358
   (library binding) | ISBN 9798765684108 (paperback) | ISBN 9798765677452 (epub)
Subjects: LCSH: Dylan, Bob, 1941-–Juvenile literature. | Singers–United States–Biography–
   Juvenile literature. | Rock musicians–United States–Biography–Juvenile literature.
Classification: LCC ML3930.D97 D64 2025 (print) | LCC ML3930.D97 (ebook) | DDC
   782.42164092 [B]–dc23/eng/20241122

LC record available at https://lccn.loc.gov/2024055927
LC ebook record available at https://lccn.loc.gov/2024055928

Manufactured in the United States of America
1-1012011-53906-3/21/2025

TABLE OF CONTENTS

Bob Dylan in 1975

The 1960s were a time of change and unrest in the United States. The Civil Rights Movement—a political and social movement for racial equality—was underway. Young people across the nation were feeling uneasy about racism and violence.

On August 28, 1963, millions of people gathered in Washington, DC, for a protest that became known as the March on Washington. Civil rights leader Martin Luther King Jr. was set to speak in front of the Lincoln Memorial. The huge crowd gathered there.

King wasn't the only one they'd come to see. Musicians had taken up the protest, and many of them were on hand to perform. Artists such as Joan Baez, Odetta, and Peter, Paul and Mary sang protest songs. But for many, the highlight of the musical performances came when twenty-two-year-old Bob Dylan performed.

Martin Luther King Jr. gives his now-famous speech, "I Have a Dream," at the 1963 March on Washington.

Dylan, with a messy mop of dark hair, stepped up with his guitar and harmonica, which he wore on a harness so he could play it hands-free. Dylan broke into a new song "When the Ship Comes In," which criticizes those in power who oppress the common people. Baez joined him to sing a backup part.

Dylan's trademark nasal vocals carried over the audience as he sang of both darkness and hope—a message that captured the gathered crowd. Dylan also sang his breakout hit, "Blowin' in the Wind," as well as "Keep Your Eyes on the Prize" and "Only a Pawn in Their Game"—a song about Black activist Medgar Evers, who had been killed by a white man.

Even before the March on Washington, Dylan had been a rising star and an icon in the Civil Rights Movement. But his profile only grew as more and more people associated him with the many changes that were sweeping the nation.

Dylan was on hand to watch King speak later. The civil rights activist gave his "I Have a Dream" speech—seen by many as the most impactful moment of the movement.

"I looked up from the podium and I thought to myself, 'I've never seen such a large crowd,'" Dylan later said. "I was up close when King was giving that speech. To this day, it still affects me in a profound way."

Dylan would go on to affect millions of others in a profound way. He was never the most musically gifted artist. He was a quirky kid with an unusual nasal tone and a complete lack of flash or showmanship onstage. But his songs cut to the heart of a restless and changing country like none other. His legend was just beginning.

Bob Zimmerman, who would later change his name to Bob Dylan, at the age of two

Minnesota Born

Bob Dylan was born Robert Allen Zimmerman on May 24, 1941, in Duluth, Minnesota. He was the first child of Abram and Beatrice Zimmerman. Later, a younger brother, David, joined the family.

Bob spent his early years in Duluth, a city on the southwestern tip of Lake Superior. When he was six years old, his father became ill with polio. The family moved about 80 miles

(129 km) west to Hibbing, Minnesota, to be nearer to his mother's family. Hibbing lies on the Mesabi Iron Range, where iron mining fuels much of the region's economy.

The Zimmerman family weren't miners, however. Abram helped run a furniture store there. As Bob grew older, he helped out in the shop. He did tasks such as sweeping the floor. His least favorite job came when someone—usually a miner—didn't have enough money to pay for the furniture they had bought on credit. Bob and other workers would have to take it back—called repossession. Bob hated it. Watching hard workers

struggle so much just to get by made a big impact on him, and it would shape his music in later years.

Young Bob didn't dream of following in his father's footsteps and making a career in the furniture business. Even as a child he showed a love of, and a talent for, music. He taught himself to play several instruments, including piano and guitar. He and his friends practiced playing songs in his garage—until neighbors complained about the noise.

From an early age, he had a distinct style. According to one of his classmates, some of his teachers discouraged him. They didn't like his unusual way of singing and playing. But one of his music teachers saw his unique talent and encouraged him. Bob sang and played with several bands, such as the Shadow Blasters and the Golden Chords, during his high school years. Bob and the Golden Chords once played at a school talent show. Their music was so loud that the school principal forced them to stop.

Bob wasn't just a performer. He was also a huge fan of music. But few radio stations reached far northeastern Minnesota. Bob didn't have access to the variety of music he wanted to hear. So his dad put an antenna on the roof of the house. It opened up new worlds to Bob, who could suddenly receive stations from Minneapolis—and sometimes as far south as Louisiana.

Bob loved cutting-edge artists such as Hank Williams and Johnnie Ray. Ray's music blended elements of blues and jazz and was part of a movement that led to a new musical style—rock and roll. Other influences included Woody Guthrie and Robert Johnson.

Johnson, a folk singer, was an inspiration. According to Zimmerman, hearing Johnson's music for the first time "had left me numb like I'd been hit by a tranquilizer bullet. . . . Over the next few weeks, I listened to it repeatedly, cut after cut, one song after another, sitting staring at the record player. Whenever I did, it felt like a ghost had come into the room, a fearsome apparition."

Bob was also a writer. He wrote stories and poems and kept them in notebooks. Those two passions—music and storytelling—led him to a growing musical style called folk.

Chasing the Dream

Bob graduated from high school in 1959. He knew that he wanted to be a musician. In his high school yearbook, he claimed that his ambition was to join rock legend Little Richard. But the path to that career was unclear. So he enrolled at the University of Minnesota in Minneapolis. He packed his bags and headed south.

He spent a year at the university. He lived in a fraternity house with other students of Jewish descent (his parents both came from Jewish families). One day in October 1959, he carried his guitar into a coffeehouse near campus called the Ten O'Clock Scholar and asked the owner if he could play. The owner agreed, and Bob took a turn on the little stage. He spent a lot of time in that coffee shop in the following months, working on his skills as a performer and learning from others who played. Around then he came up with the stage name that the world would come to know—Bob Dylan.

At the time, Dylan still had a rock style. But many of the other musicians there weren't rock singers. They favored the storytelling style of folk. As a kid, Dylan had written a lot of stories and poems, and the style of music

appealed to him. His dream began to shift. He no longer wanted to join Little Richard as a rock star. He wanted to be a folk singer instead.

After a year of college, Dylan was ready to chase that dream. He spoke to his parents about dropping out. They supported him. "He wanted to be a folk singer, an entertainer," his father said. "We couldn't see it, but we felt he was entitled to the chance. It's his life, after all, and we didn't want to stand in the way. So we made an agreement that he could have one year to do as he pleased, and if at the end of that year we were not satisfied with his progress he'd go back to school."

Not everyone was as supportive. Dylan's friends in Minneapolis thought it was a ridiculous idea. "I don't think any of us believed he was going to make it," said fellow university student Gretel Hoffman. "Because it was all so tough. Not that he wasn't good, but there were a lot of good people. And, you see, at this time he was doing very little of his own composing. Mostly singing other people's songs."

Undaunted, in January 1961, Dylan headed east to New York City. It was a bold move. Countless aspiring artists went to New York to make it big, and the vast majority of them failed. Dylan was talented and he had a vision of the artist he wanted to be. But success was far from guaranteed.

And yet Dylan quickly found an audience. Soon, he was playing in small clubs in a neighborhood called Greenwich Village. There he began to develop his sound—often just his voice with an acoustic guitar and his harmonica. In September he played in a club

Dylan plays at Gerde's Folk City in 1961.

called Gerde's Folk City, opening the show for a better-known band. *New York Times* writer Robert Shelton was in the audience to write a review of the show. He was impressed with the twenty-year-old singer and songwriter.

"Bob Dylan is one of the most distinctive stylists to play in a Manhattan [club] in months . . . there is no doubt that he is bursting at the seams with talent. . . . Dylan's voice is anything but pretty. He is consciously trying to recapture the rude beauty of a Southern field hand musing in melody on his porch. . . . His music-making has the mark of originality and inspiration, all the more noteworthy for his youth. Mr. Dylan is vague about his . . . birthplace, but it matters less where he has been than where he is going, and that would seem to be straight up."

Rapid Rise and Early Failure

The *New York Times* review was a big deal. Most of Dylan's peers had been playing clubs for years and had never enjoyed even a whisper of that kind of praise.

Around that time, popular folk singer Carolyn Hester was recording a new album for Columbia Records. She chose Dylan to play the harmonica for her. Dylan met her to play a bit. Columbia music producer John Hammond was also at the meeting. He was instantly impressed with the young artist. Hammond had Dylan sing for him, and he became more and more interested. He told Dylan that he wanted him to come to the music studio to record some demos—songs that aren't heavily produced but allow an artist to show their talents.

Folk singer and songwriter Carolyn Hester in 1965

The same day the review was published, Dylan went to Columbia Records for the recording session. Hammond's opinion of the young singer only grew. Dylan carried himself with a unique style. The way he could play guitar and harmonica and deliver his unique vocals was unlike anything Hammond had ever heard.

"So he came in and made some demos, and when I heard him I flipped," Hammond said. "I told him I wanted him to record for Columbia, and I had the contract drawn up."

Dylan understood that being a musician was all about entertainment. He wanted to be a mysterious figure. He wasn't Robert Zimmerman from Minnesota. He was Bob Dylan. When Hammond prepared the contract, he told Dylan that because he was so young, his parents needed to sign it too.

Dylan records his first album, *Bob Dylan*, at Columbia Records studios in 1961.

Dylan explained that he didn't have any parents—just an uncle who was a blackjack dealer in Las Vegas. He hadn't even recorded an album yet, but Dylan was already hard at work creating the character that he intended to become.

Dylan hurried home to show the contract to Susan Rotolo, a fellow singer who went by the name Suze. She and Dylan had been dating. Suze had been a big influence in Dylan's life since he'd arrived in New York. As he quickly gained success, she helped keep him grounded.

Dylan and his friends could hardly believe his career was taking off like it was. He'd been in New York less than a year. Most folk singers were much older. Twenty-year-old newcomers simply did not get record deals from Columbia.

Suze and Dylan in 1961

Dylan got to work choosing songs for the album. He recorded the entire thing in three recording sessions. Hammond later recalled that Dylan was very difficult to work with. Artists often record the same song over and over to get it just right. Dylan wouldn't do that. Further, his vocal style was still very raw. As Shelton had noted in his *New York Times* review, Dylan's voice was not pretty. Part of that was style. Part was inexperience.

The album, titled *Bob Dylan*, was released on March 19, 1962. It included thirteen tracks (songs), only two of which were originals—"Talkin' New York" and "Song to Woody." Columbia may have been confident in their young folk singer. But the album was a flop in sales. It was a setback, but only a minor detour in Dylan's rise to stardom.

Dylan's first album, *Bob Dylan*, was released in 1962. It didn't sell well.

Hitting It Big

In August 1962, Dylan officially changed his name to Bob Dylan. That summer he was hard at work writing songs for an upcoming second album. "I wrote a lot of songs in a quick amount of time," Dylan said of that period. "I could do that then, because the process was new to me. I felt like I'd discovered something no one else had ever discovered, and I was in a sort of an arena artistically that no one else had ever been in before ever."

One of the new songs was "Blowin' in the Wind." Its lyrics, which ask the listener a series of questions about life, war, and other topics, soon became the anthem of the American anti-war and Civil Rights Movement. "Blowin' in the Wind" would change everything for Dylan. He recorded it for his second studio album, *The Freewheelin' Bob Dylan*. The album was released on May 27, 1963. This time, audiences took notice.

Dylan performs at a folk singer holiday party in London, United Kingdom, in 1962.

"Blowin' in the Wind" marked a change in style for
Dylan. He started singing about broader themes, and the
stripped-down, personal delivery gave his lyrics an extra
sense of depth and authenticity. Other songs on the album
included "A Hard Rain's a-Gonna Fall" and "Girl from the
North Country."

Dylan's second album went on to sell more than a
million copies. And just like that, he became an icon of
the Civil Rights Movement. Dylan later said that he never
wanted that. He just wrote songs that he thought people

A civil rights demonstration in Jackson, Mississippi, in June 1963, two months before the famous March on Washington

23

would buy. But however he got there, his dreams of hitting it big had become real. Radio stations around the country were playing his songs. He was appearing on TV shows and singing in front of packed houses. Bob Dylan had arrived.

Around then, Dylan had a new love interest in his life—popular folk singer Joan Baez. While Dylan was still an up-and-comer, Baez was an established star. She did a lot to help promote Dylan. She recorded some of his songs and even invited him to appear with her onstage during her concerts. The two dated for several years before going their separate ways.

Joan Baez and Bob Dylan sing a duet at the 1963 Newport Folk Festival in Rhode Island.

JOAN BAEZ

Joan Baez had a huge influence on Dylan both personally and professionally. Baez, born January 9, 1941, hit it big with her first album, *Joan Baez* (1960). She sang in a classic folk style, with messages promoting social justice and civil rights, protesting war, and more. Among her biggest hits are "Diamonds & Rust," "Farewell, Angelina," "Love Is Just a Four-Letter Word," and Dylan's "Forever Young."

Joan Baez at the 1963 Newport Folk Festival

Searching for a Style

Dylan's profile rose in August 1963 when he performed at the March on Washington, where he shared the stage with Martin Luther King Jr. on the day of King's famous "I Have a Dream" speech. During this time, Dylan was in the middle of recording songs for his third studio album, *The Times, They Are a-Changin'*.

The album, led by the song of the same name, was released on February 10, 1964. Dylan's first two albums had featured a mix of original songs and covers—versions of songs first performed by other artists. But it had become clear that Dylan's strength was his songwriting.

So this time, there were no covers. It was all Dylan's originals.

"The Times, They Are a-Changin'" was never released as a single. But that didn't stop it from becoming an anthem for change worldwide. Dylan borrowed the melody from a Scottish ballad. He often used existing songs as inspiration for his own. Some criticized him for that, but Dylan didn't apologize.

"You use what's been handed down," he later said. "The Times, They Are a-Changin' is probably from an old Scottish folk song. I'll take a song I know and simply start playing it in my head. At a certain point, some of the words will change and I'll start writing a song."

The album was a hit, but it also marked a change that left some fans and critics uneasy.

Bob Dylan plays harmonica at the 1963 Newport Folk Festival.

Dylan's first two albums had featured a lot more variety—with lighthearted moments to balance out the serious ones. Not this one. That sense of humor and playfulness was gone. Dylan stuck to serious political songs.

Fans weren't the only ones who may have missed that other side of Dylan. His role as a civil rights icon had begun to wear on him. At times he felt trapped. People expected him to sing, speak, and behave in a certain way. Dylan was never one to do what others wanted or expected of him. Slowly, he began to reject the role that he had created for himself. He pushed against it. Not long after Lee Harvey Oswald shot and killed President John F. Kennedy in 1963, Dylan spoke at an awards ceremony. He controversially sympathized with Oswald, telling the gathered crowd that he could see a bit of himself in the assassin.

The change was apparent in his fourth album, *Another Side of Bob Dylan.* It was a complete flip from the seriousness of his previous album. It was filled with love songs and humorous lyrics, with Dylan even making fun of himself.

It was not a big surprise that the album marked a step back for Dylan's commercial success. Fans and critics wanted serious Bob Dylan, and the album didn't deliver. To no one's surprise, Dylan didn't apologize for the change.

"The songs are . . . honest . . . written only for the reason that I myself, me alone, wanted and needed to write them," he explained.

Evolving Sound

Dylan could have stuck to the simple stripped-down folk music that had made him so popular. But over the next decade, he experimented with his sound. It started with his March 1965 album *Bringing It All Back Home*. It was the first time Dylan included electrical instruments on an album.

One of the album's most popular songs was the acoustic "Mr. Tambourine Man." The melody was upbeat, and the lyrics were not as heavy as many of Dylan's earlier hits.

Dylan took his electric sound onto the stage with him. He played at the Newport Folk Festival that year with a full electric band. It didn't go well. According to some who were there, the fans hated the electric sound and even booed the star at times.

Dylan stayed busy. In August he released his second album that year. *Highway 61 Revisited* continued Dylan's more electric rock sound. The album included the smash hit "Like a Rolling Stone." The song shot to number 2 on the US charts. Popular music magazine *Rolling Stone*—whose name may have had something to do with the song—ranked it as the number 1 rock song of all time in 2010.

Dylan's busy year ended with a personal milestone. In November he and former model Sara Lownds married. Dylan adopted Lownds's daughter, Maria. The couple went on to have four children, Jesse, Anna, Samuel, and Jakob, before they divorced in 1977.

Professionally, Dylan continued to experiment. In 1967 he released his eighth album, *John Wesley Harding.* It included the song "All Along the Watchtower," which is a short conversation between a joker and a thief. Guitar legend Jimi Hendrix covered the song, giving it a huge boost in popularity.

Guitarist, singer, and songwriter Jimi Hendrix performs in San Francisco, California, in October 1968.

In 1969 Dylan took another new direction. He released *Nashville Skyline*. The album had a strong country music influence. Dylan worked with some top country stars, including the legendary Johnny Cash. Dylan and Cash teamed up on "Girl from the North Country." The two became close friends, and Dylan later appeared on the first episode of *The Johnny Cash Show*, a TV music and variety show hosted by Cash.

Dylan also experimented with a different vocal range on *Nashville Skyline*. Instead of his higher nasal tones, he sang much lower than fans were used to hearing. The vocal change was apparent on the hit single "Lay Lady Lay," among others.

The 1970s

In the 1970s, Dylan continued to delight and frustrate fans with changes in style and songwriting. Fans were

largely disappointed with his 1970 album *Self Portrait*.
Dylan kept his lower singing style from *Nashville Skyline*
on the album, which featured more covers and less
original material. Commercially, it was a flop.

Dylan later said that he'd made a bad album on
purpose. "I wish these people would just forget about me,"
he explained. "I wanna do something they can't possibly
like, they can't relate to."

Dylan appeared less and less onstage during this time.
He had grown tired of fame. He wanted to spend more
time with his kids, out of the public eye.

Music is what fueled Dylan's fame, but around this
time he explored another passion—poetry. In 1971 he
published *Tarantula*, a book of poetry. He'd written much

Dylan's book *Tarantula* was published in 1971.

of it in the previous decade, but a 1966 motorcycle accident had derailed the project. Dylan's free-form poems somewhat resembled his song lyrics, but readers were largely underwhelmed.

In 1973 Dylan's contract with Columbia Records ended. He moved to a new label, Asylum Records, and recorded *Planet Waves.* "Forever Young" was the album's biggest hit. Dylan wrote the song as a lullaby for his son Jesse, but it resonated with fans in a way that few of his recent songs had. Other artists, including Joan Baez, later released popular covers of the song.

In 1974 Dylan went on tour to support the album—his first tour in eight years. He recorded a live album, *Before the Flood,* while on tour. Neither this album nor *Planet Waves* sold well, and Dylan grew frustrated with Asylum. He returned to Columbia soon after.

Dylan tours in 1974 in support of his new album *Planet Waves*.

Later that year, Dylan recorded and released *Blood on the Tracks*. The album was heavily influenced by the challenges of his relationship with his wife, Sara. The deeply personal album went on to become a fan favorite. *Rolling Stone* listed it at number 9 on its 500 Greatest Albums of All Time list in 2020.

Salon magazine described *Blood on the Tracks* as Dylan's "only flawless album and his best produced; the songs, each of them, are constructed in disciplined fashion, written and rewritten, formed in a way his songs almost never are. It is his kindest album and most dismayed, and seems in hindsight to have achieved a sublime balance between the . . . excesses of his mid-'60s output and the self-consciously simple compositions of his post-accident years."

Dylan returned to his activist roots in 1975 with the recording of his song "Hurricane" for a new album, *Desire*, which was released the following year. The song was written in support of Black boxer Rubin "Hurricane" Carter, who had been convicted of murder. Dylan and many others believed Carter was innocent and worked to clear his name. The effort worked. Carter was later cleared of the crime.

Always Changing

Dylan grew up Jewish. But in the late 1970s, he converted to Christianity. Dylan released a series of gospel albums:

Slow Train Coming (1979), *Saved* (1980), and *Shot of Love* (1981). During this time, Dylan refused to play his old material in concert. He only played religious songs. While some loved the new direction, the sudden change of tone wasn't popular with many fans and critics.

After his brief gospel period, Dylan returned to nonreligious music. He released a stream of albums over the next decade. While some enjoyed success, his overall popularity had dipped.

Around this time, Dylan began a romantic relationship with Carolyn Dennis, one of his backup singers. The couple married in 1986 and welcomed a daughter, Desiree, later that year. They divorced in 1992.

In the late 1980s, Dylan often collaborated with other artists. He toured with Tom Petty and the Heartbreakers in 1986, often sharing the stage with Petty. Then, in 1987, he toured with the Grateful Dead. They recorded a live album together, *Dylan*

An image of Dylan from a 1986 photo shoot for *Rolling Stone* magazine

& the Dead, although it left fans of both artists mostly unsatisfied.

In 1988 Dylan was inducted into the Rock and Roll Hall of Fame in Cleveland, Ohio. Rock star Bruce Springsteen introduced him. "Bob freed your mind the way Elvis freed your body," Springsteen said. "He showed us that just because music was innately physical did not mean that it was anti-intellectual."

Left to right: George Harrison of the Beatles, Bob Dylan, Little Richard, and Mike Love of the Beach Boys perform at the 1988 Rock and Roll Hall of Fame awards ceremony.

"WE ARE THE WORLD"

In 1985 a group of musicians came together to sing "We Are the World," a song written by pop singers Michael Jackson and Lionel Richie. Dylan was among them. The song was part of a huge fundraiser to help starving people in Africa. The song was a hit and raised more than $60 million to help those in need.

That year Dylan began the Never Ending Tour. Unlike most tours, which support a specific album and last a set amount of time, the Never Ending Tour was designed to be ongoing. Since then, Dylan has continued to play shows around the world. Unlike many artists, Dylan doesn't stick to a script of must-play hits. He sings the songs he wants to sing, however he feels like singing them that night.

Dylan returned to his acoustic folk roots with a pair of albums, *Good as I Been to You* (1992) and *World Gone Wrong* (1993). He also played the popular MTV show *Unplugged*, which included fully acoustic versions of some of his classics.

In 1997 Dylan suffered from a life-threatening inflammation of tissue around his heart, caused by an infection. Dylan thought he was going to die. But he recovered and was soon back recording more music.

Later Years and Legacy

In 2001 Dylan turned sixty. He continued to make an impact on the music world. The previous year, he had written and performed the song "Things Have Changed" for the movie *Wonder Boys*. The song won an Academy Award for Best Original Song, and many count it among the best of Dylan's later career.

Dylan tried his hand at filmmaking in 2003. He cowrote and acted in the film *Masked and Anonymous*. Dylan played the role of a former rock star released from prison. The film did poorly with critics and was a flop at the box office.

Dylan continued to release a wide variety of music in the 2000s. That included a 2009 holiday album, *Christmas in the Heart*. In 2018 he recorded a song for *Universal Love: Wedding Songs Reimagined*. Dylan and other musicians recast popular wedding songs to be played at gay marriages.

In 2020 Dylan released his thirty-ninth album, *Rough and Rowdy Ways*, his first album of entirely original material in almost a decade. Fans and critics loved it. The album shot to number 1 on the *Billboard* charts. That made the seventy-nine-year-old the oldest artist ever to have a number 1 album of new material.

Unlike some artists of his generation, Dylan has embraced the internet age. He's active on several social media platforms, including Facebook—where he has nearly seven million followers—and Instagram.

Dylan's music helped to shape a generation. In the late 1990s, he appeared on the *Time* 100: The Most Important

Bob Dylan performs at a benefit concert for Farm Aid, which raised money for small family farms, in Indiana in 2023.

People of the Century list, largely because of his impact on cultural changes that swept the 1960s. But while that time period set the stage for his amazing career, it was only a part of his long story. In his eighth decade, Dylan continues to delight fans with new material and live shows.

1941   Robert Zimmerman is born on May 24 in Duluth, Minnesota.

1959   Zimmerman graduates from high school and enrolls at the University of Minnesota. He adopts the stage name Bob Dylan.

1961   Dylan goes to New York to pursue a music career.

1962   Dylan's first album, *Bob Dylan*, is released by Columbia Records.

1963   *The Freewheelin' Bob Dylan* is released. Songs such as "Blowin' in the Wind" make Dylan a star. Dylan performs at the March on Washington in August.

1965   Dylan releases *Bringing It All Back Home*, his first album to feature electrical instruments.

1969   Dylan releases the country music–themed *Nashville Skyline*.

1971   Dylan publishes *Tarantula*, a book of poetry.

1974   *Blood on the Tracks* is released, featuring songs inspired by Dylan's marriage.

1979 Dylan releases the first of three gospel albums after his conversion to Christianity.

1985 With a group of other artists, Dylan performs "We Are the World," a song to raise money for starving people in Africa.

1988 Dylan is inducted into the Rock and Roll Hall of Fame.

1996 Dylan's son Jakob and his band, the Wallflowers, release their biggest album, *Bringing Down the Horse.*

2001 Dylan wins an Academy Award for Best Original Song for "Things Have Changed."

2020 *Rough and Rowdy Ways*, Dylan's thirty-ninth album, is released.

2024 By the end of 2024, *The Essential Bob Dylan* was Dylan's most streamed album, with nearly 2.4 billion streams.

SOURCE NOTES

10 Andy Greene, "Flashback: Bob Dylan Performs at the 1963 March on Washington," *Rolling Stone*, June 9, 2020, https://www.rollingstone.com/music/music-news/bob-dylan-only-a-pawn-in-their-game-1963-martin-luther-king-1011996/.

13 Sam Kemp, "The Guitarist That Changed Bob Dylan's Life: "Like I'd Been Hit by a Tranquilliser Bullet," Far Out, August 29, 2024, https://faroutmagazine.co.uk/guitarist-changed-bob-dylans-life/.

15 Time-Life editors, *Bob Dylan* (Life Books, 2016).

16 Anthony Scaduto, "Bob Dylan: An Intimate Biography, Part One," *Rolling Stone*, March 2, 1972, https://www.rollingstone.com/music/music-news/bob-dylan-an-intimate-biography-part-one-244147/.

17 Robert Shelton, "Bob Dylan: A Distinctive Folk-Song Stylist; 20-Year-Old Singer Is Bright New Face at Gerde's Club Greenbriar Boys Are Also on Bill with Bluegrass Music," *New York Times*, September 29, 1961, https://www.nytimes.com/1961/09/29/archives/bob-dylan-a-distinctive-folksong-stylist-20yearold-singer-is-bright.html.

19 Scaduto, "Bob Dylan."

22 Alan Light, "'The Freewheelin' Bob Dylan': Inside His First Classic," *Rolling Stone*, May 27, 2016, https://www.rollingstone.com/music/music-news/the-freewheelin-bob-dylan-inside-his-first-classic-165313/.

27 Tom Poak, "60 Years Ago, Bob Dylan Recorded 'The Times They Are A-Changin'.' In 2015, He Explained How You Could Write Songs like That Too. . . ," MusicRadar.com, October 24, 2023, https://www.musicradar.com/news/bob-dylan-the-roots-of-the-times-they-are-a-changin.

28 "Writers' Revolution in Pop World," *Beat*, June 4, 1966, 6.

33 Arun Starkey, "'Self Portrait': The Album Bob Dylan Wrote to Make People Forget About Him," Far Out, January 1, 2024, https://faroutmagazine.co.uk/the-album-bob-dylan-wrote-to -make-people-forget-about-him/.

35 Bill Wyman, "Bob Dylan," Salon, May 22, 2001, https://www .salon.com/2001/05/22/dylan_3/.

37 Saeed Ahmed, "Bob Dylan Songs That Changed the Course of History (an Incomplete List)," CNN.com, October 13, 2016, https://www.cnn.com/2016/10/13/entertainment/dylan-songs -history-trnd/index.html.

SELECTED BIBLIOGRAPHY

Scaduto, Anthony. "Bob Dylan: An Intimate Biography, Part One." *Rolling Stone*, March 2, 1972. https://www.rollingstone.com/music /music-news/bob-dylan-an-intimate-biography-part-one-244147/.

Shelton, Robert. "Bob Dylan: A Distinctive Folk-Song Stylist; 20-Year-Old Singer Is Bright New Face at Gerde's Club Greenbriar Boys Are Also on Bill with Bluegrass Music." *New York Times*, September 29, 1961. https://www.nytimes.com/1961/09/29/archives/bob-dylan-a -distinctive-folksong-stylist-20yearold-singer-is-bright.html.

Sounes, Howard. *Down the Highway: The Life of Bob Dylan.* Grove Atlantic, 2011.

Starkey, Arun. "'Self Portrait': The Album Bob Dylan Wrote to Make People Forget About Him." Far Out, January 1, 2024. https:// faroutmagazine.co.uk/the-album-bob-dylan-wrote-to-make-people -forget-about-him/.

Wilentz, Sean. *Bob Dylan in America.* Random House, 2011.

Wyman, Bill. "Bob Dylan." Salon, May 22, 2001. https://www.salon .com/2001/05/22/dylan_3/.

LEARN MORE

Britannica Kids: Bob Dylan
https://kids.britannica.com/kids/article/Bob-Dylan/399435

Gigliotti, Jim. *Who Was Johnny Cash?* Penguin Workshop, 2022.

Green, Meghan. *The Story of the American Civil Rights Movement.* Cavendish Square, 2024.

Morall-Baker, Dr. Monica B. *Hip-Hop and Social Justice: Rhymes of Resistance.* Lerner Publications, 2026.

The Official Bob Dylan Site
https://www.bobdylan.com

Rock and Roll Hall of Fame: Bob Dylan
https://rockhall.com/inductees/bob-dylan/

PHOTO ACKNOWLEDGMENTS

Image credits: H. Thompson/Evening Standard/Hulton Archive/Getty Images, p. 2; Everett Collection Historical/Alamy, p. 6; Bettmann/Getty Images, p. 8; Rowland Scherman/Getty Images, pp. 9, 24, 25, 27; ARCHIVIO GBB/Alamy, pp. 10, 12; Jenn Ackerman For The Washington Post via Getty Images, p. 11; dpa/Alamy Live News, p. 15; Michael Ochs Archives/Getty Images, pp. 17, 19, 20, 29, 34; Popperfoto via Getty Images, p. 18; Hugh Williamson/Alamy, p. 21; Brian Shuel/Redferns via Getty, p. 22; Daily Express/Pictorial Parade/Archive Photos/Getty Images, p. 23; Stocktrek Images, Inc./Alamy, p. 26; Charlie Steiner - Highway 67/Getty Images, p. 30; Mira/Alamy, p. 31; Alan Wilson/Alamy, p. 33; Aaron Rapoport/Corbis via Getty Images, p. 36; Ebet Roberts/Redferns via Getty Images, p. 37; Pictorial Press Ltd/Alamy, p. 38; Gary Miller/Getty Images, p. 41.

Cover: Everett Collection Historical/Alamy.